עם

TABLET II

NAME: _______________________________

I will stand my watch
And set myself on the rampart,
And watch to see what He will say to me,
And what I will answer when I am corrected.
Then the Lord answered me and said: "Write the vision
And make *it* plain on tablets,
That he may run who reads it.
Habakkuk 2:1-2 (New King James Version)

This is the second edition of My Tablet. It includes all new quotes or prompts that I receive during my study of God's Word. It is my hope that you'll use this journal to document your visions and goals that the Lord has placed in your heart. Believing that they will surely come to pass.

Dr. Kevin Abankwa

Understanding the knowledge of God's Word brings about the effectual manifestation of his Word in your life.

Date: ___ / ___ / _____

Counsel in the heart of man *is like* deep water,
But a man of understanding will draw it out.
Proverbs 20:5 [NKJV]

Understanding is the soil that carries the seed of knowledge.

Date: ___ / ___ / _____

Date: ___ / ___ / _____

A scoffer seeks wisdom and does not *find it,*
But knowledge *is* easy to him who understands.
Proverbs 14:6 [NKJV]

The knowledge of God's word can only be put to effectual use through understanding.

Date: ___ / ___ / _____

When anyone hears the word of the kingdom, and does
not understand *it,* then the wicked *one* comes and
snatches away what was sown in his heart. This is he who
received seed by the wayside.
Matthew 13:19 [NKJV]

*The planting of the seed of the Word in a
human heart produces fruits of faith.*

Date: ___ / ___ / _____

Date: ___ / ___ / _____

So then faith *comes* by hearing, and hearing by the word
of God.
Romans 10:17 [NKJV]

Question everything through the lens of God's Word, for it is the means by which everything in this universe is born, regulated and sustained.

Date: ___ / ___ / _____

All things were made through Him, and without Him
nothing was made that was made.
John 1:3 [NKJV]

Always look for the evidence. Even the unseen things the Lord provides evidence of their existence.

Date: ___ / ___ / _____

Date: ___ / ___ / _____

Now faith is the substance of things hoped for,
the evidence of things not seen.
Hebrews 11:1 [NKJV]

Believing hinges on knowledge, what knowledge fuels your beliefs?

Date: ___ / ___ / _____

Date: ___ / ___ / _____

Every believer should be a "miner" in Christ.

Date: ___ / ___ / _____

Date: ___ / ___ / _____

Always hold truth in righteousness.

Date: ___ / ___ / _____

Date: ___ / ___ / _____

For the wrath of God is revealed from heaven against all
ungodliness and unrighteousness of men, who suppress
the truth in unrighteousness.
Romans 1:18 [NKJV]

The perfection of a fruit bearing tree is to bring forth good fruits in its season.

Date: ___ / ___ / _____

Date: ___ / ___ / _____

Correction and sustenance produces comfort.

Date: ___ / ___ / _____

Date: ___ / ___ / _____

Yea, though I walk through the valley of the shadow of
death, I will fear no evil; For You *are* with me;
Your rod and Your staff, they comfort me.
Psalm 23:4 [NKJV]

Refuse to be ignorant of the present truth of God's Word. Your growth depends on it.

Date: ___ / ___ / _____

Date: ___ / ___ / _____

For this reason I will not be negligent to remind you
always of these things, though you know and are
established in the present truth.
2 Peter 1:12 [NKJV]

Miracles don't just happen, they are worked out.

Date: ___ / ___ / _____

Date: ___ / ___ / _____

To another the working of miracles, to another prophecy,
to another discerning of spirits, to another *different* kinds
of tongues, to another the interpretation of tongues.
1 Corinthians 12:10 [NKJV]

Date: ___ / ___ / _____

Date: ___ / ___ / _____

This Book of the Law shall not depart from your mouth,
but you shall meditate in it day and night, that you may
observe to do according to all that is written in it. For then
you will make your way prosperous, and then you will have
good success.
Joshua 1:8 [NKJV]

As you increase in the knowledge of God, you also increase in the knowledge of His will.

Date: ___ / ___ / _____

Date: ___ / ___ / _____

That you may walk worthy of the Lord, fully
pleasing *Him,* being fruitful in every good work and
increasing in the knowledge of God.
Colossians 1:10 [NKJV]

If you want to change the scenery, you have to change the sound.

Date: ___ / ___ / _____

Then God said, "Let there be light"; and there was light.
Genesis 1:3 [NKJV]

Faith is a vector quantity, having both speed and direction.

Date: ___ / ___ / _____

Date: ___ / ___ / _____

Then Jesus said to the centurion, "Go your way; and as
you have believed, *so* let it be done for you." And his
servant was healed that same hour.
Matthew 8:13 [NKJV]

Understand the thoughts of God and you won't misinterpret His hand.

Date: ___ / ___ / _____

Date: ___ / ___ / _____

For I know the thoughts that I think toward you, says
the Lord, thoughts of peace and not of evil, to give you a
future and a hope.
Jeremiah 29:11 [NKJV]

You can't change what you avoid, you cannot impact what you don't want to be a part of.

Date: ___ / ___ / _____

Date: ___ / ___ / _____

Another parable He spoke to them: "The kingdom of
heaven is like leaven, which a woman took and hid in
three measures of meal till it was all leavened."
Matthew 13:33 [NKJV]

If you know the concepts of His Word you cannot misinterpret the facts in His Word.

Date: ___ / ___ / _____

Date: ___ / ___ / _____

Or do you not know, brethren (for I speak to those who
know the law), that the law has dominion over a man as
long as he lives?
Romans 7:1 [NKJV]

Until you learn how to walk, running becomes a hazardous act.

Date: ___ / ___ / _____

Date: ___ / ___ / _____

For everyone who partakes *only* of milk *is* unskilled in the
word of righteousness, for he is a babe.
Hebrews 5:13 [NKJV]

Don't be dried up, meditate on the Word.

Date: ___ / ___ / _____

Date: ___ / ___ / _____

He shall be like a tree
Planted by the rivers of water,
That brings forth its fruit in its season,
Whose leaf also shall not wither;
And whatever he does shall prosper.
Psalms 1:3 [NKJV]

Character is built on knowledge. The accurate knowledge that you have determines the excellence of your character.

Date: ___ / ___ / _____

And this I pray, that your love may abound still more and
more in knowledge and all discernment, that you may
approve the things that are excellent, that you may be
sincere and without offense till the day of Christ,
Philippians 1:9-10 [NKJV]

*Always look for the wind behind the waves
and address it.*

Date: ___ / ___ / _____

Date: ___ / ___ / _____

Then He arose and rebuked the wind, and said to the
sea, "Peace, be still!" And the wind ceased and there was a
great calm.
Mark 4:39 [NKJV]

What you honor, you attract.

Date: ___ / ___ / _____

Date: ___ / ___ / _____

He who receives a prophet in the name of a prophet shall
receive a prophet's reward. And he who receives a
righteous man in the name of a righteous man shall receive
a righteous man's reward.
Matthew 10:41 [NKJV]

*These three will always prove your maturity:
speech, understanding, and thoughts.*

Date: ___ / ___ / _____

Date: ___ / ___ / _____

When I was a child, I spoke as a child, I understood as a
child, I thought as a child; but when I became a man, I put
away childish things.
1 Corinthians 13:11 [NKJV]

An accepted truth is a practiced truth.

Date: ___ / ___ / _____

Date: ___ / ___ / _____

Let your light so shine before men, that they may see your
good works and glorify your Father in heaven.
Matthew 5:16 [NKJV]

To trust in God is to lean, establish and rest
your mind on Him always.

Date: ___ / ___ / _____

You will keep *him* in perfect peace,
Whose mind *is* stayed *on You,*
Because he trusts in You.
Trust in the Lord forever,
For in Yah, the Lord, *is* everlasting strength.
Isaiah 26:3-4 [NKJV]

The full manifestation of knowledge is in understanding.

Date: ___ / ___ / _____

Date: ___ / ___ / _____

So that
'Seeing they may see and not perceive,
And hearing they may hear and not understand;
Lest they should turn,
And *their* sins be forgiven them.
Mark 4:12 [NKJV]

There is no true authority without a restraining principle.

Date: ___ / ___ / _____

I will worship toward Your holy temple,
And praise Your name
For Your lovingkindness and Your truth;
For You have magnified Your word above all Your name.
Psalm 138:2 [NKJV]

The proof of any claim is in its testing.

Date: ___ / ___ / _____

Date: ___ / ___ / _____

Focus on the spirit, address the spirit and the physical follows suite.

Date: ___ / ___ / _____

Then He arose and rebuked the wind, and said to the
sea, "Peace, be still!" And the wind ceased and there was a
great calm.
Mark 4:39 [NKJV]

To be spiritually minded is to be scripturally minded.

Date: ___ / ___ / _____

Date: ___ / ___ / _____

For those who live according to the flesh set their minds on
the things of the flesh, but those *who live* according to the
Spirit, the things of the Spirit.
Romans 8:5 [NKJV]

You don't know wrong until right is defined.

Date: ___ / ___ / _____

Date: ___ / ___ / _____

I was alive once without the law, but when the
commandment came, sin revived and I died.
Romans 7:9 [NKJV]

As your mind is a gateway, so is your heart the storehouse.

Date: ___ / ___ / _____

Date: ___ / ___ / _____

For as he thinks in his heart, so *is* he.
"Eat and drink!" he says to you,
But his heart is not with you.
Proverbs 23:7 [NKJV]

Date: ___ / ___ / _____

Date: ___ / ___ / _____

A dry hill can never hold water, but a dry valley will not stay dry for long when the water comes.

Date: ___ / ___ / _____

Date: ___ / ___ / _____

Date: ___ / ___ / _____

Date: ___ / ___ / _____

So that you come short in no gift, eagerly waiting for the
revelation of our Lord Jesus Christ.
1 Corinthians 1:6 [NKJV]

For you are still carnal. For where *there are* envy, strife,
and divisions among you, are you not carnal and behaving
like *mere* men?
1 Corinthians 3:3 [NKJV]

Date: ___ / ___ / _____

Date: ___ / ___ / _____

For since the creation of the world His
invisible *attributes* are clearly seen, being understood by
the things that are made, *even* His eternal power and
Godhead, so that they are without excuse.
Romans 1:20 [NKJV]

Our calling is not chosen by us, but He chooses us for His purpose and we answer Him.

Date: ___ / ___ / _____

Date: ___ / ___ / _____

Now the Lord came and stood and called as at other times,
"Samuel! Samuel!"
And Samuel answered, "Speak, for Your servant hears."
1 Samuel 3:10 [NKJV]

Date: ___ / ___ / _____

Date: ___ / ___ / _____

He teaches my hands to make war,
So that my arms can bend a bow of bronze.
Psalm 18:34 [NKJV]

*Faith is like a fingerprint, it's unique to you
and responses to only you. You cannot
"share" it with anyone.*

Date: ___ / ___ / _____

Date: ___ / ___ / _____

If you know the concepts of His Word you cannot misinterpret the facts in His Word.

Date: ___ / ___ / _____

Date: ___ / ___ / _____

These things He said, and after that He said to them, "Our
friend Lazarus sleeps, but I go that I may wake him up."
John 11:11 [NKJV]

It takes humility for Life to be subjected to death temporarily for the sake of love.

Date: ___ / ___ / _____

Date: ___ / ___ / _____

And being found in appearance as a man, He humbled
Himself and became obedient to *the point of* death, even
the death of the cross.
Philippians 2:8 [NKJV]

Everything that the Lord has placed in your authority functions by your understanding.

Date: ___ / ___ / _____

Date: ___ / ___ / _____

Therefore my people will go into exile
for lack of understanding;
those of high rank will die of hunger
and the common people will be parched with thirst.
Isaiah 5:13 [NIV]

The anointing is made efficient in a believer
by knowledge.

Date: ___ / ___ / _____

Date: ___ / ___ / _____

The hypocrite with *his* mouth destroys his neighbor,
But through knowledge the righteous will be delivered.
Proverbs 11:9 [NKJV]

Don't only be a sower, but also a partaker of the bread.

Date: ___ / ___ / _____

Date: ___ / ___ / _____

Now may He who supplies seed to the sower, and bread
for food, supply and multiply the seed you have *sown* and
increase the fruits of your righteousness.
2 Corinthians 9:10 [NKJV]

The success of a creation can only be defined by its creator.

Date: ___ / ___ / _____

Date: ___ / ___ / _____

Before I formed you in the womb I knew you;
Before you were born I sanctified you;
I ordained you a prophet to the nations.
Jeremiah 1:5 [NKJV]

A perfect man is the one that can identify the gift, the giver of the gift, and to differentiate between the presence of the two.

Date: ___ / ___ / _____

Date: ___ / ___ / _____

Gifts can be deceptive but the fruits bear witness to truth.

Date: ___ / ___ / _____

Date: ___ / ___ / _____

A good tree cannot bear bad fruit, nor *can* a bad tree bear
good fruit.
Matthew 7:18 [NKJV]

Date: ___ / ___ / _____

And you shall know the truth, and the truth shall make you free.
John 8:32 [NKJV]

The seed of faith received from the Father, is dependent on the knowledge of his Word.

Date: ___ / ___ / _____

Date: ___ / ___ / _____

"For I say, through the grace given to me, to everyone
who is among you, not to think *of himself* more highly than
he ought to think, but to think soberly, as God has dealt to
each one a measure of faith.
Romans 12:3 [NKJV]

Revelation is progressive because knowledge is progressive, and the glory of His illumination is ever increasing.

Date: ___ / ___ / _____

Date: ___ / ___ / _____

But the path of the just *is* like the shining sun,
That shines ever brighter unto the perfect day.
Proverbs 4:18 [NKJV]

The Word of God is absolute truth, and the revelations thereof is ever increasing day by day.

Date: ___ / ___ / _____

Date: ___ / ___ / ______

For this reason I will not be negligent to remind you always
of these things, though you know and are established in
the present truth.
2 Peter 1:12 [NKJV]

Salvation is the beginning, not the end.

Date: ___ / ___ / _____

Who desires all men to be saved and to come to the
knowledge of the truth.
1 Timothy 2:12 [NKJV]

His provisions in their entirety, collectively are sufficient.

Date: ___ / ___ / _____

Date: ___ / ___ / _____

So He said to them, "This kind can come out by nothing
but prayer and fasting."
Mark 9:29 [NKJV]

You study the Word to make it yours.

Date: ___ / ___ / _____

These were more fair-minded than those in Thessalonica,
in that they received the word with all readiness,
and searched the Scriptures daily *to find out* whether these
things were so.
Acts 17:11 [NKJV]

Whatever you need; give.

Date: ___ / ___ / _____

Date: ___ / ___ / _____

Who gave Himself for us, that He might redeem us from
every lawless deed and purify for Himself *His* own special
people, zealous for good works.
Titus 2:14 [NKJV]

If you destroy your roots, you can never bear fruits.

Date: ___ / ___ / _____

Date: ___ / ___ / _____

For if the firstfruit *is* holy, the lump *is* also *holy;* and if the
root *is* holy, so *are* the branches. And if some of the
branches were broken off, and you, being a wild olive tree,
were grafted in among them, and with them became a
partaker of the root and fatness of the olive tree, do not
boast against the branches. But if you do boast, *remember
that* you do not support the root, but the
root *supports* you.
Romans 11:16-18 [NKJV]

The Lord has planted the seed of Life in our Spirit. To produce the fruits of Life.

Date: ___ / ___ / _____

Date: ___ / ___ / _____

The fruit of the righteous *is a* tree of life,
And he who wins souls *is* wise.
Proverbs 11:30 [NKJV]

If you cannot bear the written Word how much more can you handle the revelations that proceeds fourth from it?

Date: ___ / ___ / _____

Date: ___ / ___ / _____

As also in all his epistles, speaking in them of these things,
in which are some things hard to understand, which
untaught and unstable *people* twist to their own
destruction, as *they do* also the rest of the Scriptures.
2 Peter 3:16 [NKJV]

Date: ___ / ___ / _____

Date: ___ / ___ / _____

Date: ___ / ___ / _____

Date: ___ / ___ / _____

Date: ___ / ___ / _____

Date: ___ / ___ / _____

INDEX

29.

30.

31.

32.

33.

34.

35.

36.

37.

38.

39.

40.

41.

42.

43.

44.

45.

46.

47.

48.

49.

50.

51.

52.

53.

54.

55.

56.

57.

58.

59.

60. ____
61. ____
62. ____
63. ____
64. ____
65. ____
66. ____
67. ____
68. ____
69. ____
70. ____
71. ____
72. ____
73. ____
74. ____
75. ____
76. ____
77. ____
78. ____
79. ____
80. ____
81. ____
82. ____
83. ____
84. ____
85. ____
86. ____
87. ____
88. ____
89. ____
90. ____

91. ____
92. ____
93. ____
94. ____
95. ____
96. ____
97. ____
98. ____
99. ____
100. ____
101. ____
102. ____
103. ____
104. ____
105. ____
106. ____
107. ____
108. ____
109. ____
110. ____
111. ____
112. ____
113. ____
114. ____
115. ____
116. ____
117. ____
118. ____
119. ____
120. ____
121. ____

122.

123.

124.

125.

126.

127.

128.

129.

130.

ABOUT THE AUTHOR

Dr. Kevin Abankwa is passionate for the knowledge of God's Word. Born in Accra, Ghana he loved the Lord from a young age and his knowledge of God's Word has only grown over the years. Through this journal he shares some of the thoughts the Spirit of God gives him as he studies the Word of God. Kevin is a chemical engineer, data & analytics expert, and entrepreneur. He earned his doctoral degree in business administration – data analytics at Grand Canyon University. He lives in North Carolina, USA with his wife and three children.

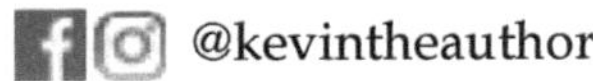 @kevintheauthor

Email: kevintheauthor2020@gmail.com

www.ingramcontent.com/pod-product-compliance
Lightning Source LLC
Chambersburg PA
CBHW020839150726
48196CB00002B/126